SHAPING MODERN SCIENCE

What Are Newton's Laws of Motion?

Denyse O'Leary

Crabtree Publishing Company

www.crabtreebooks.com

SHAPING MODERN SCIENCE

Author: Denyse O'Leary
Publishing plan research and development:
  Sean Charlebois, Reagan Miller
  Crabtree Publishing Company
Editors: Sara Goodchild, Adrianna Morganelli
Proofreaders: Kristine Lindsay, Molly Aloian
Project coordinator: Kathy Middleton
Editorial services: Clarity Content Services
Production coordinator and prepress technician:
  Katherine Berti
Print coordinator: Katherine Berti
Series consultant: Eric Walters
Cover design: Katherine Berti
Design: First Image
Photo research: Linda Tanaka
Photographs: cover/title page Shutterstock; p4 left Brett Mulcahy/
iStock, Kirk Strickland/iStock; p5 Ben Blankenburg/iStock; p6 Josef Philipp/
iStock; p7 Anthony Baggett/Dreamstime.com; p8 Detail of The School of
Athens by Raffaello Sanzio, 1509, showing Plato (left) and Aristotle (right)/
public domain/wiki; p9 Atlas, New York City/public domain/wiki; p10 Bust
of Aristotle. Marble, Roman copy after a Greek bronze original by Lysippos
from 330 BC/public domain/wiki; p10–11 Lindamore/Dreamstime; p11
Cpbackpacker/Shutterstock; p12 Archimedes Thoughtful by Domenico Fetti
original in Alte Meister Museum Dresden Germany/public domain/wiki; p13
Public domain/wiki, from Chambers's Encyclopedia (Philadelphia: J. B.
Lippincott Company, 1875); p14 essxboy/iStock; p15 Pius Lee/Shutterstock;
p16 top Portrait of Galileo Galilei by Justus Sustermans (1597-1681)/public
domain/wiki, Asky/Dreamstime.com; p18 top paulrdunn/iStock, Public
domain/wiki; p19 De Nobilitatibus Sapientii Et Prudentiis Regum Manuscript/
public domain/wiki; p20 Galileo Galilei showing the Doge of Venice how to
use the telescope, currently in the Bertini Room, Villa Andrea Ponti, Italy/
public domain/wiki; p21 NASA-JPL-Caltech-Steward/O. Krause, et al; p22
Galileo facing the Roman Inquisition painting by Cristiano Banti/public
domain/wiki, Gustaf Brundin/iStock; p26 Public domain/wiki; p27 Dimitar
Marinov/iStock; p28 top From National Inventory of Scientific Instruments
by Charles Mollan, Royal Dublin Society, number 3699 ARM012 Orrery
Armagh Observatory, Zhukov Oleg/Shutterstock; p29 VladisChern/
Shutterstock; p30–31 Mirvav/Shutterstock; p32 Gerardo Burgos Galindo/
Shutterstock; p34 Chandra Ganegoda; p35 Vittorio Bruno/Shutterstock; p36
Lasse Kristensen/Shutterstock; p37 Dylan Kereluk from White Rock, Canada
licensed under the Creative Commons Attribution 2.0 Generic license; p38
Francesco Ridolfi/Shutterstock; p39 Bruce Works/Shutterstock; p40 Brady
Holt Creative Commons Attribution 3.0 Unported license; p41 Péter Gudella/
Shutterstock; p42 Joggie Botma/Shutterstock; p43 get4net/Shutterstock; p44
Sportlibrary/Shutterstock; p45 james steidl/iStock; p46 Vuk Vukmirovic/
iStock; p47 Yasonya/Shutterstock; p48 U.S. Air Force photo/Airman 1st
Class Nadine Y. Barclay/public domain; p49 Pedro Salaverria/Shutterstock;
p50 Janaka Dharmasena/Shutterstock; p51 Kayros Studio/Shutterstock;
p52 Spigget licensed under the Creative Commons Attribution-Share Alike
3.0 Unported license; p53 H. Raab licensed under the Creative Commons
Attribution-Share Alike 3.0 Unported license; p54 Portrait by Ferdinand
Schmutzer/public domain/wiki; p55 NASA; page 56–57 Stephen Sweet/
iStock; p57 NASA.

Library and Archives Canada Cataloguing in Publication

O'Leary, Denyse
    What are Newton's laws of motion? / Denyse O'Leary.

(Shaping modern science)
Includes index.
Issued also in an electronic format.
ISBN 978-0-7787-7200-2 (bound).--ISBN 978-0-7787-7207-1 (pbk.)

    1. Newton, Isaac, Sir, 1642-1727--Juvenile literature.
2. Motion--Juvenile literature. 3. Gravity--Juvenile literature.
I. Title. II. Series: Shaping modern science

QA803.O43 2011   531'.1   C2011-900178-0

Library of Congress Cataloging-in-Publication Data

O'Leary, Denyse.
    What are Newton's laws of motion? / Denyse O'Leary.
        p. cm. -- (Shaping modern science)
    Includes index.
    ISBN 978-0-7787-7200-2 (reinforced lib. bdg. : alk. paper)
    -- ISBN 978-0-7787-7207-1 (pbk. : alk. paper) --
    ISBN 978-1-4271-9529-6 (electronic PDF)
    1. Motion--Juvenile literature. I. Title. II. Series.

QC127.4.O44 2011
531'.11--dc22

                                        2010052629

Crabtree Publishing Company

www.crabtreebooks.com   1-800-387-7650

Printed in the U.S.A./022011/CJ20101228

**Published in
Canada
Crabtree Publishing**
616 Welland Ave.
St. Catharines, ON
L2M 5V6

**Published in the
United States
Crabtree Publishing**
PMB 59051
350 Fifth Avenue, 59th Floor
New York, New York 10118

**Published in the
United Kingdom
Crabtree Publishing**
Maritime House
Basin Road North, Hove
BN41 1WR

**Published in
Australia
Crabtree Publishing**
386 Mt. Alexander Rd.
Ascot Vale (Melbourne)
VIC 3032

Contents

What Are the Laws of Motion?

A soccer player kicks the ball into the net, scoring the winning goal. Roller coaster riders gasp and scream as the coaster slowly reaches the top of the first hill, then plummets at dizzying speed.

A snowboarder wows spectators with bold flips and turns. **Motion** is everywhere. The cells of our bodies, the planets of our solar system, and everything between, are full of things in motion.

The world is full of things in motion.

Describing Motion

Two sets of scientific laws describe motion. One set is called **classical mechanics**. This set describes the motion of objects we see every day. The other is called **quantum mechanics** (also known as quantum physics). Quantum mechanics takes effect on the scale of the very, very tiny particles that make up atoms. In this book, we look at classical mechanics and its founder: Isaac Newton (1642–1727).

Laws and Theories: What's the Difference?

A **scientific law** is a statement that describes a pattern in nature. It may be a statement in words, a mathematical equation, or both. Albert Einstein's $E = mc^2$ is a law that describes the relationship between **energy (E)**, **mass (m)**, and the speed of light (c). A law describes what happens. It does not explain why. For that, you need a theory.

A **scientific theory** is an explanation for an event or events that occur in the natural world. For an explanation to be accepted as a theory, it must be supported by a great deal of evidence. Until then it is called a **hypothesis**. For example, the Big Bang theory says the universe started as a single point 13 billion years ago. The point expanded and cooled quickly. It continues to expand today. This theory is an explanation for how the universe began and what it is like today. It is supported by a great deal of evidence.

Quick fact

Most pioneers in the study of motion were called "natural philosophers." The term "scientist" was first recorded in 1834.

What Does Classical Mechanics Do?

Classical mechanics is based on the study of **forces**. A force acts on a body (an object) and may cause it to move. When you throw a ball, you provide the force that moves it. When the wind blows away a sheet of newspaper, the wind provides the force. We have all experienced the effects of forces. Classical mechanics is a way to understand, study, and use them. Classical mechanics describes forces and the motion of objects in terms of Newton's three laws of motion and his law of universal gravitation. What are these laws?

Newton's Laws of Motion

1. The law of **inertia**: objects in motion stay in motion and objects at rest stay at rest unless some force acts on them.
2. The law of **acceleration**: a force acting on an object changes its motion in a predictable way that can be expressed using an equation.
3. The law of action and reaction: for every action there is an equal and opposite reaction.

Newton's Law of Universal Gravitation

Every object in the universe attracts every other object. The force of attraction is called **gravity** and its strength depends on the masses of the objects involved and the distance between them.

These laws will be explored more fully in later chapters.

← This toy, called a Newton's Cradle, is an example of the laws of motion in action.

Why Are Newton's Laws So Important?

Newton once said that he could see clearly how motion works because he stood "on the shoulders of giants." These earlier scientist "giants" were researching specific areas. Nicolaus Copernicus (1473–1543) developed a model of the solar system that showed the planets, including Earth, orbiting the Sun. Galileo Galilei (1564–1642) demonstrated a number of facts about motion via his experiments. Johannes Kepler (1571–1630) developed laws for the motion of planets. René Descartes (1596–1650) created mathematical tools that scientists could use.

These scientists and the ancient thinkers who came before them all brought us closer to an understanding of motion. But what tied it all together into a single picture was Newton's laws of motion in 1687. They described motion simply, clearly, and mathematically. They applied equally on Earth and throughout the solar system.

His laws are still important today, whether people are using classical mechanics to design better snowboards, to build more exciting roller coasters…or to explore the universe.

←This statue of Isaac Newton stands at Trinity College at Cambridge University.

"I do not know what I may appear to the world, but to myself I seem to have been only like a boy playing on the sea-shore, and diverting myself in now and then finding a smoother pebble or a prettier shell than ordinary, whilst the great ocean of truth lay all undiscovered before me."

— Isaac Newton

CHAPTER ONE

Investigating the World

It seems likely that people have always puzzled over the motion of objects on Earth and in the sky. For much of human history, we can only guess at peoples' ideas about why and how things move. But five thousand years ago, something changed—writing was invented. People could communicate over time and space. Even today we can learn about their ideas.

Ancient Greeks and the Motion of the Planets

The philosophers of ancient Greece studied the motion of the planets 2,300 years ago. They hoped that these planets could tell them more about Earth. In fact, most people believed in **astrology**. They believed they could predict and explain events on Earth by studying the planets.

↑ This 1509–1510 painting by Raphael shows Plato (left) and his student Aristotle (right).

It was early days for the science of **astronomy**. The telescope had not yet been invented 2,300 years ago. People could see only the planets visible to the unaided eye: Mercury, Venus, Mars, Jupiter, and Saturn. They could not know that there were other planets or dwarf planets beyond those. They could see the stars, but they could not know the vast size of the universe.

Plato

The philosopher Plato (428–348 B.C.) taught that the planets, the Sun, and other stars (heavenly bodies) circled the Earth. Earth was fixed in place in the center of the system. Plato thought that the heavenly bodies moved in circles because the circle was a perfect shape. The planets other than Earth, the Sun, and other stars were considered perfect and unchanging.

Aristotle

Plato's student Aristotle (384–322 B.C.) taught that the heavenly bodies moved because rotating spheres carried them.

Aristotle became very well known. His ideas about motion were accepted for about two thousand years.

Explaining Nature through Myth

Philosophers investigated their world through logic and reasoning. This was not the only way for people to understand nature, though. The Greek myths were religious stories that explained how and why things happened. The stories usually featured gods, kings, heroes, and ordinary people.

According to one myth, the gods wanted to punish a dull-witted but strong giant, Atlas. His punishment was to hold up the sky. Atlas tried to trick the hero Hercules into doing it instead. But Hercules outsmarted him and fled. This story answered the question, *why doesn't the sky fall to Earth?*

Mythic explanations are different from scientific explanations. They express people's feelings about themselves and nature. Scientific explanations are based on observation and experiment.

How Did Aristotle Think Motion Occurred?

Aristotle thought that Earth was not like the other, perfect planets. On those planets, he believed, there was no change, death, or decay. Earth, in contrast, was heavy and material. It experienced change and decay.

Aristotle's theory of motion explained that things fall down toward Earth because, like Earth, they are heavy and material. He believed that "like attracts like." Falling objects were just finding their natural home. Only unchanging and perfect things were pure and light enough to remain in the region beyond the Moon.

↑Aristotle's ideas and methods helped shape modern science thousands of years later.

Aristotle's Four Elements

Aristotle also taught that nature consists of four "**elements**." His elements were earth, water, air, and fire. He explained their motion in terms of their differing "heaviness." Earth (solid materials) and water are heavy. They fall toward Earth. But a stone can pass through water, so a stone must be heavier than water. Air moves up away from Earth because it is light. Bubbles pass up through water, for example. Fire shoots up because it is lightest of all.

Quick fact

Scientists today have a different meaning for element. They have so far identified at least 118 elements. Aristotle's element water is made of two of today's elements: hydrogen and oxygen.

How Aristotle Explained the Motion of Water

In his essay *Meteorology*, Aristotle explained the water cycle:

> Now the sun, moving as it does, sets up processes of change and becoming and decay, and by its agency the finest and sweetest water is every day carried up and is dissolved into vapor and rises to the upper region, where it is condensed again by the cold and so returns to the earth.

In today's terms, Aristotle was saying that energy from the Sun causes water to evaporate and rise. Then cold air condenses it, and it falls back to Earth as rain.

Apart from the fact that Earth orbits the Sun (not the reverse), Aristotle's explanation is generally correct. It assumes that nature follows laws that can be studied and described. This is a central idea of modern science. That is why, 2,500 years later, Aristotle is honored as one of the founders of science.

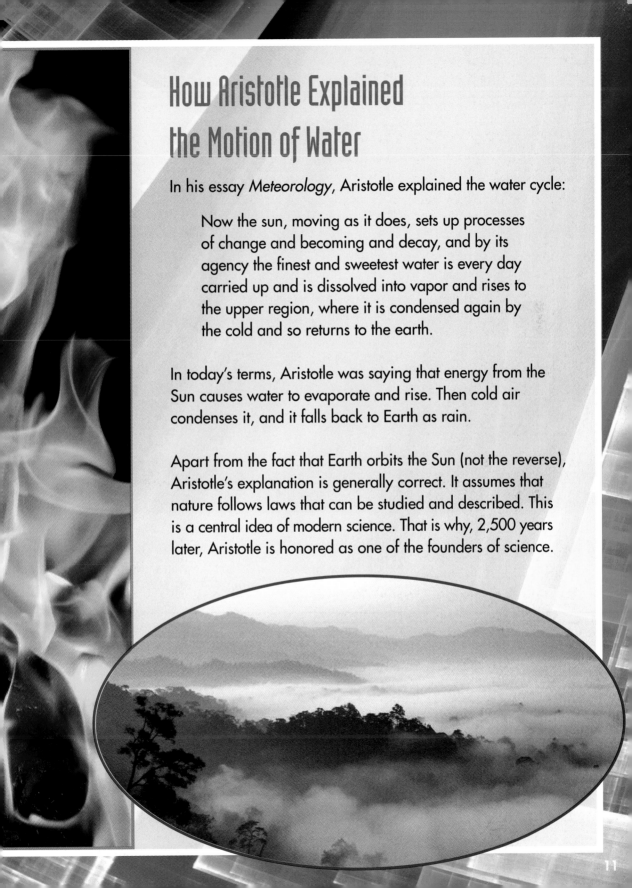

Other Early Greek Thinkers

Aristotle and the Greek thinkers who followed are remembered for some remarkable achievements in science.

Pythagoras

Pythagoras (c. 580–500 B.C.) formulated the Pythagorean **theorem**. This theorem made the calculation of heights possible.

Euclid

Euclid (c. 330–260 B.C.) developed the mathematical system that geometry relies on today.

Eratosthenes

Eratosthenes (276–194 B.C.) measured the circumference of Earth quite accurately for his time. He also tried to measure the distance to the Moon and Sun.

↑ *Legend has it that Archimedes came up with his famous principle in the bathtub.*

Archimedes

The mathematician Archimedes (c. 287–212 B.C.) is best remembered for Archimedes' principle. People had long noticed that things seem lighter in water than in air. Also, some things float and some sink. But was there a law behind these observations? Archimedes learned through experiment that, a floating object displaces its own **weight** of the fluid in which it floats. He also explained why some things float and others sink in water.

Archimedes' Screw

Archimedes improved on the hydraulic screw, an Egyptian invention used to raise water from one level to another. The hydraulic screw is an example of a technology that used motion before the laws of motion were understood.

A spiral fits inside a cylinder open at both ends. The lower end sits under water at an angle and the upper end has a handle to turn the spiral. The rotating spiral traps and raises water.

Quick fact

When Archimedes thought of his principle, he ran through the streets shouting *"Eureka!"* meaning "I have found it." We still use this ancient Greek word today to celebrate a discovery.

"We. . .must take for granted that the things that exist by nature are, either all or some of them, in motion."

— Aristotle

Egyptian Innovations

The Greek philosophers were not the only people who left evidence of their thinking in their writings. About 3000 B.C., the Egyptians began writing. This information could be shared widely over centuries. In fact, we can read Egyptian **hieroglyphs** today.

Egyptians also developed a way to write large numbers. They wrote the largest parts of a number before the smaller ones, arranged in order. Large numbers were important for keeping track of the rise and fall of the water levels of the Nile River. The Nile was hugely important to Egyptian society. Their crops depended on the river's water. Life depended on keeping track of its flow from year to year.

What about motion on Earth and above? While building huge structures like the pyramids, the Egyptians learned a great deal about motion. For example, they developed canals, ramps, wedges, and scaffolding to move huge stones for building. They developed these technologies through trial and error.

↑ *These hieroglyphic numbers are found in the Karnak Temple in Luxor, Egypt.*

Like the Greeks, the Egyptians studied the skies. Egyptians considered the year to have three seasons. These were the Nile's flooding, its subsiding, and the harvest. They divided each of these seasons into four 28-day cycles of the Moon. For that reason, their year came out to only 336 days, not 365. They solved this problem by waiting until the calendar fell so far behind that the star Sirius, known to rise in the twelfth month, rose very late. Then they would add a thirteenth month.

Making Sense of Motion

About 2,500 years ago, people began to ask important questions about motion. A question like "Why do things fall down and not up?" may seem silly. It is not a silly question at all, though. Something *causes* them to fall. What is that something? Science is about asking these kinds of questions. Why didn't people ask much earlier? Perhaps because, tens of thousands of years ago, motion chiefly meant the motion of complex life forms, like animals. There were too many factors to consider.

Things changed when simple machines such as the wheel and axle, bow and arrow, ramp, and wedge became popular. Societies developed these technologies by trial and error to solve problems, such as how to carry heavy objects or how to better defend territory. But some thinkers also began to use these devices to try to make sense of motion.

← *The ancient Egyptians must have used simple machines such as ramps to build their massive pyramids.*

CHAPTER TWO

Galileo and the Science of Motion

Galileo Galilei (1564–1642) was the eldest of seven children. His father wanted him to study medicine, but he was drawn to experiments, discoveries, and inventions.

Galileo made his first scientific discovery while he was a reluctant 20-year-old medical student. Observing a swinging lamp, he wondered how long the lamp took for long and short swings. He used his pulse to time the swings. He found that the time elapsed for each swing was the same. Later, his observations became the **law of the pendulum**.

The law of the pendulum (1583) started Galileo's career. He soon abandoned medicine for mathematics, securing an appointment to the University of Pisa, and later, Padua.

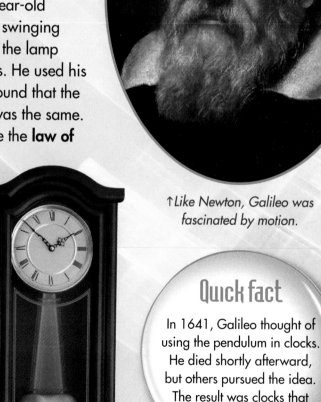

↑ *Like Newton, Galileo was fascinated by motion.*

Quick fact

In 1641, Galileo thought of using the pendulum in clocks. He died shortly afterward, but others pursued the idea. The result was clocks that were more accurate.

Challenging Ancient Ideas

In Galileo's day, scientists tended to accept ancient ideas, such as Aristotle's, as fact. This tendency troubled Galileo. He wanted to test theories by observation and experiment. When he did, his findings disproved some widely accepted theories.

Over the years, Galileo built equipment and performed many experiments. These experiments helped him challenge traditional ideas about motion. For example, he rolled balls on a ramp (inclined plane) with a gentle slope, then judged the balls' motion at equal time intervals. He concluded that all objects fall at the same speed. During the fall, the speed increases in the same predictable way.

Galileo's theory was very different from Aristotle's theory. Aristotle had taught that like attracts like. He thought balls and other objects fall because they seek the "heavy" Earth. Most people concluded that heavier objects *must* therefore fall faster. Galileo's experiment proved that theory incorrect. It also showed why experiment is critical to science.

A Job for the Moons of Jupiter

A problem that faced sailors in Galileo's day was how to determine longitude at sea. Many shipwrecks resulted from wrong guesses. Galileo argued that eclipses of Jupiter's moons might serve as guides. If the person viewing the eclipse compared the time the eclipse would be observed in, say, Lisbon, with the time the ship's clock gave, longitude could be determined.

Galileo's method could not work in his day. There was not accurate enough data about the eclipses of his newly discovered moons. Also, accurate enough clocks did not exist. By the 1760s, both problems were solved. The famed Mason–Dixon line (1763–1767) separating northern and southern states was determined in part by observing Jupiter's moons.

Did You Know?
Wind **drag** affects how fast things fall. A feather and a rock fall at the same speed in airless conditions.

What Goes Up Must Come Down

Galileo studied **projectiles**, such as balls, for many years. Ancient thinkers held that a single inner force, which they called the impetus, influences the ball. The ball moves in a straight line until the impetus runs out. Then it falls straight downward.

Observation shows, however, that the ball actually falls in a smooth curve. Using his inclined plane, Galileo showed that two motions, not one, influence the ball. The force of gravity pulls the ball down. But the ball also continues to move forward. He saw that, without gravity, the ball would simply continue on the same course at the same speed.

Galileo wanted a mathematics-based solution to the ball's movement. He graphed it as a **parabola**, which is a curve that can be described with a mathematical equation. Galileo's work with projectiles was an important building block for Newton as he developed his laws of motion.

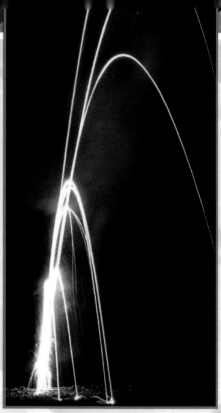

↑ *These firework sparks rise and fall in the shape of parabolas.*

↑ *These cannons are from the 1500s.*

Galileo Fires Up Ballistics

The earliest muskets, made during the 1300s, were very inefficient. This was due to early trial-and-error technology. Guns improved over the centuries, though. By Galileo's day, cannons dominated warfare. Once people could be sure that a ball would go where they aimed it, an accurate understanding of ballistics (projectile motion) became essential.

Some of Galileo's Other Scientific Ideas

Galileo was mostly interested in experimenting. Still, he sometimes developed theories. For example, in 1624, he started a book that explained the tides of the ocean in terms of the motion of Earth. The movements of the seas, he argued, are due not to a mystical attraction between the moon and the water, as many believed. Instead they are due to other mechanical causes. Galileo was right about the mechanical causes. But he was mistaken in thinking that Earth's motion alone caused it. Newton later showed that the gravitational interaction between Earth and the Moon causes tides. Galileo also considered the question of why rolling objects stop. He reasoned that a force called **friction** stops them. When a ball rolled down one of a pair of inclined planes facing each other, he observed that it would roll up the opposite one, to about the same height. The smoother the plane, the closer the ball got to its original height. The difference between the original and the final heights, he reasoned, was the result of friction. Without friction, the ball would reach exactly the same height on the other side. Newton built on this idea, too.

↑ *This image of an early cannon dates from 1329.*

Galileo's Many Inventions

Galileo designed a hydrostatic balance (1586) that could show that a piece of gold was 19.3 times as heavy as the volume of water it displaced.

Later, he invented a variety of devices to sell because he needed money for his family:

- a military compass (1596) that aimed cannonballs accurately
- a modified version of the compass (1597), suited to surveying land
- a water thermometer (1606) that could measure temperature changes accurately

But then he started making big changes in astronomy, and not everyone was happy about it.

Galileo's "Spyglass" Reveals an Unsettling New Universe

While vacationing in Venice in 1609, Galileo heard of a newly invented Dutch device that made far-off objects seem near. The device was then called a spyglass (only later a telescope). It was treated as a military secret.

Not a man to be easily discouraged, Galileo quickly built a telescope himself, and began to watch the night sky. He was well rewarded, for in 1610, he observed the phases of Venus, the craters on the Moon, and the moons of Jupiter. Meanwhile, he mapped some star formations. In 1611, he and other astronomers also saw sunspots.

↓ *This painting depicts Galileo (standing) demonstrating his telescope for a nobleman of Venice (seated).*

Why Were Galileo's Ideas Challenging?

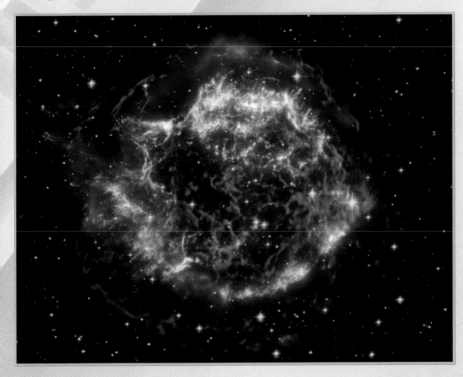

← When Galileo observed a supernova, he realized that objects in the sky were not perfect and unchangeable.

When Galileo and other astronomers used telescopes to identify previously unknown features of our solar system, their discoveries profoundly affected their culture.

Galileo observed features that the revered ancient thinkers did not know of. Many new findings conflicted with long-held ideas. For example, if the Moon was pure, why did it have craters? If Venus was unchangeable, why did it have phases?

Then, on October 10, 1604, a supernova (a very bright exploding star) was first sighted in Padua. Galileo saw it on December 24. He then gave three lectures at the University of Padua, pointing out that, contrary to ancient theories, even the stars can change.

Quick Fact

Galileo observed structures around Saturn that suggested a triple star system. Later observers, with more powerful telescopes, realized that the structures were in fact rings.

Galileo and the Inquisition

In 1543, natural philosopher Nicolaus Copernicus published a book that argued that the Sun, not Earth, was the center of the solar system. Galileo supported Copernicus's model at a time when many viewed it with suspicion. They were far more comfortable with Aristotle's Earth-centered view. The challenges most people experienced were easily explained by the material heaviness and imperfection of Earth, compared to the perfect heavenly bodies. But what if the whole universe was imperfect?

A devout Catholic Christian, Galileo did not see any conflict between faith and Copernicus's model. But the Catholic Church, the most powerful institution in Galileo's culture, worried about what uneducated people might assume.

At first, relations were friendly. The Pope, an old friend, gave Galileo a pension—and advised him to be cautious. Galileo was watched closely by the Inquisition, an arm of the Church that determined correct doctrine. The Inquisition could ban a book, and jail, torment, and execute its author.

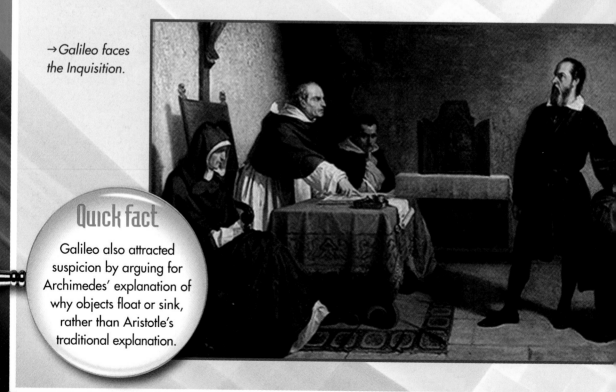

→ Galileo faces the Inquisition.

Quick fact

Galileo also attracted suspicion by arguing for Archimedes' explanation of why objects float or sink, rather than Aristotle's traditional explanation.

↑With a view from space, it is easier to understand that Earth orbits the Sun.

Galileo Under Arrest

Galileo was told he could represent Copernicus's model only as a hypothesis, that is, a testable idea about how nature works. But Galileo continued to insist that Copernicus was right. Finally, by 1616, he was told not to believe, discuss, or defend the Copernican model. He could still say it was a hypothesis. But when he finished his *Dialogue Concerning the Two Chief World Systems* in 1630, it became clear he truly thought it was fact.

In 1632, Galileo was summoned to Rome and interrogated, under threat of torture. In 1633, he pleaded guilty to a lesser charge and publicly declared that he was wrong to maintain Copernicus's theory as fact. He remained under house arrest for life, though he continued to observe, experiment, and publish until his death in 1642. In 1992, the Catholic Church apologized for its treatment of Galileo. Today, the Inquisition goes by a different name and is responsible only for religious matters.

"In questions of science, the authority of a thousand is not worth the humble reasoning of a single individual."

— Galileo Galilei

CHAPTER THREE

Laying Down the Law

Isaac Newton (1642–1727) was one of the greatest scientists of all time. Like Albert Einstein, he is a widely recognized figure. But his beginnings were humble and difficult.

Newton was born in Lincolnshire, England. His father had died three months before his premature birth. His mother married again and moved away, leaving Newton with his grandparents. Asking and answering questions about the world around him helped Newton deal with his loneliness. When his mother returned years later as a widow, she insisted that he should leave school and become a farmer. The headmaster of Newton's school protested, though, and he was allowed to continue his schooling. Newton left for Cambridge University in 1761.

↑Newton was 46 when this portrait was painted. He was already famous for his achievements.

Newton's Apple

Newton once told a friend that falling apples helped him develop a law of gravitation. Popular illustrations sometimes show an apple hitting his head and inspiring him. Whether or not the story is true, it took Newton a lot of hard work to turn inspiration into the laws we know and use today.

Using Equations to Describe Nature

Newton is best known for his mathematical explanations of motion and of light. Many scientists of his day were close to understanding the forces behind motion. But they expressed their ideas in slightly different ways, so confusion resulted. Newton, a mathematician, realized that consistent statements and equations were needed.

For this purpose, he clearly defined concepts such as mass, inertia, force, and acceleration. He carried out experiments and developed equations to show how those concepts were all related. In doing so, he extended Galileo's work on motion by introducing the three laws of motion. These laws provided a scientifically sound account of motion after centuries of dispute.

Isaac Newton:
The Man Who Put It All Together

Newton showed early promise in mathematics and physics, evident in his brilliant student notes. He was elected Lucasian Professor of Mathematics in 1669 when he was 27. In addition to his work in science, he served as a member of Parliament twice, at a time of crisis and controversy. King James II had been deposed and foreign monarchs, William and Mary, were crowned to replace him. He also served as Master of the Mint until his death in 1727, where he showed considerable skill at detecting and eliminating **counterfeit** money.

A famous poet wrote a tribute intended for his tomb:

"Nature and Nature's laws lay hid in night:
God said, "Let Newton be!" and all was light."

— Alexander Pope

Why Is Newton Considered One of the Greatest Scientists of All Time?

Newton brought together key discoveries and combined them to create a unified view of the universe and its physical laws. His three laws of motion applied to large and small objects everywhere. Underlying them was the principle of gravity, a universal attractive force exerted between any two bodies. His laws form the basis of classical mechanics, the set of rules that describe how objects in motion behave.

→ *The full name of Newton's most famous work is Philosophiae Naturalis Principia Mathematica. That title means Mathematical Principles of Natural Philosophy.*

Newton's laws simplified physics and encouraged scientists to observe, research, and experiment. Still, not everyone was happy with the "clockwork" view of the universe that his laws suggested.

"If I have seen further it is by standing on the shoulders of giants."

—Isaac Newton

PHILOSOPHIÆ
NATURALIS
PRINCIPIA
MATHEMATICA.

Autore JS. NEWTON, Trin. Coll. Cantab. Soc. Matheseos Professore Lucasiano, & Societatis Regalis Sodali.

IMPRIMATUR.
S. PEPYS, Reg. Soc. PRÆSES.
Julii 5. 1686.

LONDINI,
Jussu Societatis Regiæ ac Typis Josephi Streater. Prostat apud plures Bibliopolas. Anno MDCLXXXVII.

Gravity and the *Principia*

Why was Newton so interested in the apple falling? He wanted to know what holds the planets in orbit. Why don't they just fall into the Sun? For that matter, why doesn't the Moon fall into the Sun, as an apple falls to Earth? After studying the problem, he offered his explanation of the mathematical principles of motion in the *Principia* (1687). This book in three volumes was the high point of Newton's career. It set out his three laws of motion and his law of universal gravitation.

Today, we take the idea of gravity for granted. But Newton's law of gravitation was not immediately accepted. One problem was that he could not identify a mechanism by which gravity works. His response to critics was that he did not know what causes gravity and would not pretend to. He did suggest that unseen particles might cause it.

Even without a theory to explain it, his law became accepted because other scientists found it reliable for predicting orbits and for measuring and representing the Earth and its gravity.

Gravity's cause is still unknown. Today, some physicists agree with Newton that a particle called a graviton causes gravity's attractive force, though they have not yet identified one.

The Solar System as One Giant Clock

Newton's model of the solar system (considered at the time to be the whole universe) seemed to explain everything. One result was that many scientists began to think of the universe as a precise clock, with many wheels revolving in perfect time. Everything was entirely predictable in this model, including all human behavior. Many people doubted such sweeping conclusions. Could Newton's laws really describe the whole universe?

Quick fact

Astronomer Johannes Kepler (1571–1630) observed that the planets move around the Sun in ellipses, not Copernicus's circles. His corrections made the Sun-centered system a more accurate and widely accepted model.

↑An orrery, like the one shown here, is a clockwork model of the solar system.

No More Problems to Solve?

The clock was a natural model of the universe at a time when clocks and watches were becoming more common and important in everyday life. Many thought Newton's laws could indeed describe everything in the universe. In 1900, one of Britain's leading scientists, William Thomson Kelvin (1824–1907), even said that physics was running out of problems to solve.

Just then two dark clouds appeared on the horizon of classical Newtonian mechanics. Recent measurements of the speed of light and the behavior of some types of radiation did not seem to follow Newton's laws. Kelvin was certain that these troublesome clouds would be blown away shortly. In fact, all of modern physics—**relativity** and quantum mechanics—began with these clouds. Newton wasn't wrong in what he observed or the conclusions he drew.

But nature, it turned out, had some laws other than Newton's.

He did not, as many hoped, provide a complete explanation of how nature works. But he did provide a picture that greatly advanced science and that is still useful today. It is worth keeping in mind that he lived during a time of civil war. In his lifetime, one king of England was beheaded and another deposed. For anxious thinkers, he provided a picture of the world that made sense.

"To explain all nature is too difficult a task for any one man or even for any one age. 'Tis much better to do a little with certainty, and leave the rest for others that come after you, than to explain all things by conjecture without making sure of any thing."

— Isaac Newton

CHAPTER FOUR

The Three Laws

How did Newton's laws of motion become the foundation of classical mechanics? An in-depth look will help us see how the laws allowed people to make sense of the universe. Newton's three laws, and the concept of gravity that underlies them, explained a great deal of the world around us. They continue to enable many advances in science and technology.

The First Law of Motion (The Law of Inertia)

Picture the bike rack at a school. The bikes are not moving. Newton would say that they are motionless. His first law says they will stay motionless because no force is pulling or pushing them.

Now school is over and some students pull their bikes out of the rack. The students' arms are providing the force that moves the bicycles. Then the students ride the bikes home. The students' legs provide the force that gets them going and keeps them moving.

So far, it seems pretty straightforward. But here is where Newton's first law gets interesting. What happens when a student stops pedaling? The bicycle will coast along for a while, but eventually, it will stop. This seems natural enough, until you stop to wonder: Why, exactly, does the bike stop?

The bike needed force to get started. So why did it stop with no apparent force applied?

"A state of rest" means not moving. "Uniform motion" means moving at a constant speed in one direction. A force must act on a motionless bike to get it moving. Likewise, a force must act on a bike in motion to stop it. Otherwise, it would just keep going.

In fact, a force does act on the bike to make it stop: friction. We'll learn more about friction later. If you could ride your bike in conditions with no friction, wind, or other force to make it stop, such as outer space, the bike would go on essentially forever once it was in motion.

The First Law and Outer Space

Outer space is almost a **vacuum**. A vacuum is an area that contains practically no matter at all. If an object is set in motion in space, there is no force to stop it. Unless it collides with a planet or the Sun, it will just keep going. This is why it is important for astronauts working on the outside of the International Space Station to remain tethered to the station! So the motion of an object does not change unless a force acts on it. Is there a way to quantify (express in numbers) how forces change the motion of objects? This is exactly what Newton's second law does.

Quick fact

The first law is often called the law of inertia. That term can be confusing because, in everyday language, inertia means doing nothing. In physics, it means *changing* nothing.

The Second Law of Motion (The Law of Acceleration)

Newton's first law states that an object changes its motion only when a force acts on it. But it does not say exactly how the force changes the object's motion. The second law makes it possible to calculate the relationships among force, acceleration, and mass.

We all know by experience that the heavier an object is, the harder the challenge of getting it moving and keeping it moving, let alone making it move faster. Think of the difference between pushing an empty shopping cart and a full one.

Picture a racecar. When the race starts, the force provided by burning fuel in the engine accelerates the car from 0 mph (0 m/s) to its desired speed. The driver controls the force provided by the engine by pushing the gas pedal. More gas means more force. More force means increased acceleration. Suppose another racecar has twice the mass of the first. Then twice the force is needed to provide the same acceleration.

↓ The greater the mass of a racecar, the more force is needed for a given acceleration.

Newton's second law of motion says:

Force (*F*) and acceleration (*a*) are **directly proportional**. The greater the force, the greater the acceleration, given the same mass. But mass (*m*) and acceleration are **inversely proportional**. The more mass, the less acceleration, given the same force.

Newton expressed this idea as an equation: $F = ma$.

Mass, Acceleration, and Force

- Mass means the quantity of matter in a substance. Unlike **weight**, mass is not affected by gravity. A racecar would weigh less on the Moon than on Earth. Its mass would not change. We'll learn more about weight in the next chapter.

Quick fact

Formula One cars are required to weigh at least 1367 lbs (620 kg).

- Acceleration is the change in an object's **velocity** (speed and direction) over time.
  In science, that change can be an increase or a decrease. Speeding up and slowing down are both acceleration in scientific terms. Acceleration is usually expressed as "distance per second per second." Let's say that a ball is dropped from a bridge. It accelerates at a rate of 32 feet per second per second (9.8 m/s^2). That is, it increases its speed by 32 feet per second (9.8 m/s) with each second that it falls.

- The unit of measurement for force is the **newton (N)**. A force of one newton (1 N) will accelerate a mass of 1 kilogram at the rate of 1 meter per second per second (2.2 lbs 39 in/s^2).

The Third Law of Motion
(The Law of Action and Reaction)

Have you heard the expression, "For every action there is an equal and opposite reaction?" It is a statement of Newton's third law of motion. Another way of putting it is this: if an object is pushed or pulled, it will push or pull to an equal extent in the opposite direction.

Quick fact

When you hit a ball with a tennis racket, the racket slows down. The ball pushes back on the racket with an equal but opposite force to the hit.

Picture a horse pulling a cart with a heavy load. The horse acts as a force on the cart in one direction. But the cart also acts as a force on the horse in the opposite direction. The cart moves forward because it is on wheels, while the horse's hooves have grip.

Suppose the horse was on roller blades and the cart's wheels were removed. If the horse pushed the cart with its nose, the cart would push back with an equal but opposite force. The horse would move backward on the roller blades.

You can experience the third law for yourself if you push off from the boards at a skating rink. You exert a force on the boards, and the boards push back equally at you.

↓ *Picture a horse and cart to visualize action and reaction in motion.*

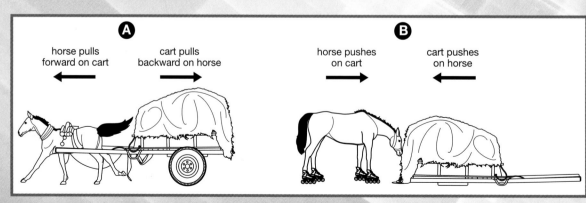

A

horse pulls forward on cart ← cart pulls backward on horse →

B

horse pushes on cart → ← cart pushes on horse

Newton's third law of motion says:
When one object exerts a force on another object, the second object exerts an equal but opposite force on the first.

Action and Reaction Under Water

When an octopus moves through the water, it relies on Newton's third law. It takes in and then squirts out water. When the squirt hits the surrounding water, the surrounding water pushes back on the squirt. The force of the water's pushback propels the octopus forward.

Beyond the Three Laws

Before Newton, astronomer Johannes Kepler had already developed laws that described the planets' paths and positions. In fact, he was the first astronomer to observe that the planets orbit in ellipses (ovals), not circles. But his laws did not explain why they followed those paths at those positions.

Other astronomers asked, why didn't the planets all just sail out in a row, past the Sun and into the stars? Why did they remain in orbit? In addition to the three laws of motion, Newton's *Principia* also proposed a universal law of gravitation. That law could describe and predict the movements of the planets.

The Law of Universal Gravitation

Newton's major goal was to link together many related recent findings and set out a general law that applied to all parts of the universe. He was especially interested in finding a way to account for the planets' orbits.

In the *Principia*, Newton introduced the law of universal gravitation.

Also, the force of gravity decreases when the distance between objects increases. The effect of distance on gravity is greater than the effect of mass. That is why objects on Earth fall toward Earth and not toward the Sun. The Sun is much, much more massive than the Earth, but it is much farther away, too.

> Newton's law of universal gravitation says:
> Gravity is an attractive force between all objects with mass, in all parts of the universe. The force of gravity is directly proportional with the product of the two masses. The force of gravity is inversely proportional with the square of the distance between them.

In other words, the effects of gravity increase with mass but decrease with distance. Large objects have a greater attractive force than small objects. That is why gravity on the surface of the Moon is much smaller than gravity on the surface of Earth.

↑ *Knowing how to calculate the effects of gravity is essential for space travel.*

Gravity and Tides

Galileo thought that Earth's movement caused tides. That was a reasonable hypothesis. But Newton provided the accepted explanation in the *Principia*. When the Moon's gravity pulls Earth, it also pulls the water on its surface. It pulls hardest on the side facing the Moon, pulling the water closer to itself. The pull is weakest on the side that faces away from the Moon, so that water stays behind. All this pulling stretches both the Earth and its water, resulting in two bulges on opposite sides of the Earth.

harbor at high tide

harbor at low tide

Let's go back to the orbits of the planets. The Sun's gravity acts on all of the planets, keeping them in orbit. The planets don't just crash into the Sun because they also have forward motion. This motion started when the solar system was formed. The balance between the Sun's gravity and the forward motion of each planet results in the orbit of each planet. In the *Principia*, Newton worked out equations that allow scientists to calculate anything from the acceleration of a falling apple to the best orbit by which a spacecraft could reach Mars. But there was, and still is, much more to learn about motion.

CHAPTER FIVE

Mass and Weight

Newton's first law of motion introduced the concept of inertia: an object at rest remains at rest and an object in motion remains in motion, unless a sufficiently strong force acts on it. The mass of the object and the nature of its motion determines what "sufficiently strong" means. One force that commonly changes the motion of objects is gravity. In this chapter, we'll explore inertia, mass, and the effects of gravity.

→ The weightlifter must counteract the inertia of the barbell and control its motion.

Inertia

For at least 2,000 years, scientists assumed that an object has a natural tendency to stay at rest and that force is needed to move it. Without force being continuously applied, they thought, the object would go back to its "natural" state of rest.

That is why, even today, most people use the word inertia to mean resistance to motion, but not resistance to rest. We say that a rock lying on the ground is inert. We do not tend to say that about a rock moving through space at a constant velocity (speed and direction). Yet the space rock really is inert, because it shows no change in its motion.

Mass and Inertia

Mass is the quantity of matter a body contains, regardless of its size or any forces acting on it. Mass and inertia depend on each other. The more massive the object, the greater its inertia. A stopped train requires a lot of force to start. Once started, it requires a lot of force to stop. We can also turn the idea around and predict that an object that shows great inertia has great mass.

Do Gases Have Mass?

Aristotle thought that air did not have mass. In fact, gases such as those in air do have mass. But unlike solids, their mass is spread out over a huge space. In other words, they have a very low **density**. So their mass went unnoticed for many centuries.

If you have felt the difference between picking up a full and empty propane tank, you have felt for yourself that a gas has mass.

The mass of a gas is easier to observe when it is compressed. Compressed oxygen turns into a liquid, which is stored at a very low temperature ($-274°F/-134°C$) to prevent its escape. If a 100 lb (45.4 kg) cylinder of liquid oxygen were released at room temperature, it would soon be 8,917 gallons (33,751 L) in volume! It would have the same mass, but over a much greater volume, and with much lower density.

Quick fact

Galileo started working on the concept of inertia in his inclined plane experiments. He reasoned that if he could prevent all friction, the balls would just roll on.

Momentum

We say our favorite sports team has momentum when it is on a winning streak. In science, the term **momentum** is used a bit differently. It is a measurement of mass in motion.

Momentum depends on two quantities: mass and velocity. Velocity is speed in a given direction. If we multiply the mass of an object by its velocity, we get its momentum.

If an object is moving, its mass and velocity are equally important for determining momentum. A bird flying swiftly along the highway has small mass and large velocity. A heavily loaded truck traveling at the same speed has large mass and a large velocity. Therefore, the truck has more momentum than the bird. Of course, if the truck stopped, its momentum would decline to 0 mph (0 m/s), and then any bird in flight would have more momentum than the truck.

↓Car manufacturers crash test new models to check how safe they are in collisions.

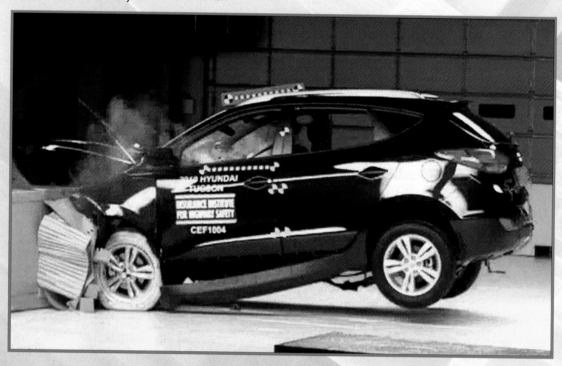

Momentum and Collisions

What happens when two objects collide? Consider one billiard ball hitting another. The two balls in play exert a force on each other, and their motion changes. Their momentum is conserved, though. According to the law of conservation of mass, the system has the same momentum before and after the collision. That means that the sum of the momentum of the balls before the collision is the same as the sum after the collision.

Suppose a white billiard ball in motion hits a red billiard ball at rest straight on. If the white ball stops, the red ball continues with the same velocity that the white ball had. (The masses of the balls do not change, of course.)

Quick fact

A racecar travels at a steady speed around an oval-shaped racetrack. Is its velocity constant as well? No. The car is constantly changing direction.

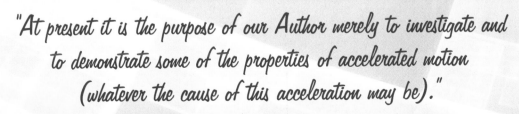

"At present it is the purpose of our Author merely to investigate and to demonstrate some of the properties of accelerated motion (whatever the cause of this acceleration may be)."

— Galileo Galilei

Mass versus Weight

It is easy to confuse the terms "mass" and "weight," but they are very different. Weight is relative, but mass is not. The weight of an object is due to the downward force of gravity pulling on it. If an object has a certain mass on Earth, it will still have the same mass on Mercury or Jupiter. But its weight will be very different, depending on the surface gravity of each planet.

Weight on Other Planets

Let's say Kayla has a mass of 80 lbs (36.3 kg). That means she weighs 80 lbs (360 N) here on Earth. On Mars, Kayla would weigh 30 lbs (130 N) and on Jupiter, 203 lbs (900 N). On the Sun, Kayla would weigh a whopping 2,232 lbs (9,900 N). That's almost twice the minimum weight for a Formula One racecar here on Earth! Kayla's mass would not change, but her weight (the downward force of gravity) certainly would. Weight is a question of *where* you are, but mass is a question of *what* you are.

Quick fact

The imperial system of measurement uses pounds for both mass and weight. On Earth, one pound of butter is both its mass and weight. On the Moon, the butter would weigh about 0.2 lbs. Its mass would still be one pound.

Gravity

Objects traveling in space, such as comets, satellites, and planets, are not affected by many different kinds of forces because space is a vacuum. But they are affected by the gravity of planets and stars. Remember that gravity depends on two things. It depends on the masses of two objects and the distance between them.

Sometimes we hear the expression "zero gravity." Although it probably expresses quite well how a person floating in space feels, it is not strictly accurate. Stars attract other stars and galaxies attract other galaxies across the universe. So there is no such thing as zero gravity anywhere in the universe. But gravity's force gets smaller with distance. That's why the force created by a vast far-off galaxy may produce no detectible change in the motion of, say, an apple aboard the International Space Station.

Center of Gravity

The average location of the weight of an object (the downward force that gravity exerts) is called its **center of gravity**. The location of an object's center of gravity affects its stability. For example, racecars have low centers of gravity to prevent them from flipping over on tight turns. A motorcycle has a higher center of gravity and a small base. It tips over easily when not in motion.

Did You Know?

Many forces in the universe, such as electric and magnetic forces, both attract and repel. For example, the magnetic North Pole attracts this compass needle. Gravity is different. It always attracts; it does not repel.

Cavendish and Earth's Mass

An experiment with a pair of lead spheres (1798) allowed English physicist Henry Cavendish (1731–1810) to establish Earth's mass, based on the mass required to produce its gravity.

friction and Energy

friction

Friction is a force that works against the direction of motion. For example, if you push a boat over sand toward a lake, the force of friction acts in the direction away from the lake.

What causes friction? Friction is caused by the attraction of solid surfaces to one another. This attraction occurs at the molecular level. The roughness or smoothness of a surface can also affect friction. Rough surfaces usually create greater friction than smooth surfaces. But even seemingly smooth surfaces such as glass or ice appear rough when viewed under a microscope.

Friction is the force that resists motion, but it is essential for many types of motion. We need friction in order to walk safely, for example. A custodian places a caution sign in front of a newly washed floor because wet patches reduce the floor's friction, making falls more likely.

Quick fact

Scientists doubt that truly friction-free surfaces are realistically possible. They develop low-friction surfaces instead. One example is the coatings used on nonstick pans for cooking.

←The high pressure between ice and an ice skate melts the ice. Skaters are actually skating on a thin layer of water, reducing the effects of friction.

Drag

Drag is a force that is similar to friction. It acts in the direction opposite to motion. The difference is that friction involves contact between two solid objects, and drag involves contact between a solid object and a liquid or gas. Like friction, drag impedes movement. Cars, aircraft, and watercraft are streamlined to minimize the effects of drag.

Drag and friction both waste energy. Note that "waste" does not mean the same thing as "destroy." According to the law of conservation of energy, energy cannot be destroyed. But drag and friction transform useful energy into **thermal energy**, which usually just escapes into the environment as heat. Much fuel is burned to overcome drag and friction when operating vehicles.

Experts suggest keeping bike and car tires inflated to conserve energy. Keeping tires inflated reduces friction by reducing the surface area that contacts the road. Experts also suggest driving with as few windows as possible open, to streamline the car and thus reduce drag.

Quick fact

On bike trips, smart cyclists ride in a line, not a swarm. The lead cyclist reduces the drag for the other cyclists. Cyclists can take turns leading the pack.

Did You Know?

Friction is both good and bad for cars. Tires need friction to grip the road, for example. But in an engine, friction damages moving parts. Using motor oil reduces the friction.

Work

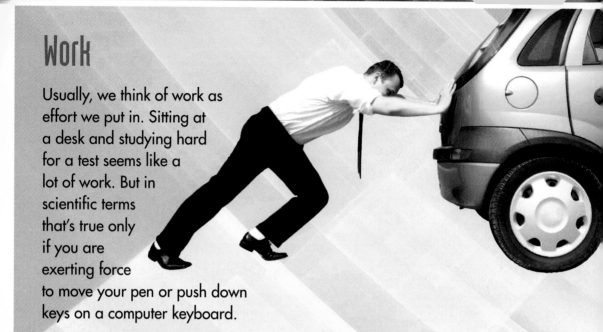

Usually, we think of work as effort we put in. Sitting at a desk and studying hard for a test seems like a lot of work. But in scientific terms that's true only if you are exerting force to move your pen or push down keys on a computer keyboard.

When talking about the physics of motion, **work** only happens if something moves. Physicists say that work is force exerted over a distance. If you roll a stalled car off the highway, you've done work. If you push hard but can't move the car, you haven't done any work. In physics, work equals force times distance. If the car didn't move, the distance it moves, and the work you did, equals zero.

Thomas Young: Work and Energy

A British scientist, Thomas Young (1773–1829), was the first to use the term "energy" (1807) as it is understood today. For "work," in the physics sense, he used the term "labor expended." He noted in a lecture that "labor expended" was not proportional to momentum but to the energy obtained.

Young is best known for demonstrating in 1803, via a double slit experiment, that light travels as waves. (Newton was convinced that light energy travels as particles.) Young's finding hinted at twentieth-century quantum mechanics.

Energy

The ability to do work is called energy. Energy comes in many forms, and often changes from one form to another. For example, the electrical energy carrying the signal in headphones becomes sound energy that you can hear. Electrical energy in a lightbulb becomes light energy, and in heating elements it becomes thermal energy (heat).

The engines in vehicles burn fuel to get the energy they need to move. Similarly, your body uses energy to move. Food is the fuel your body "burns" to generate the energy it needs to move you.

Forms of Energy

Energy takes many forms, including
- thermal energy (heat)
- light
- electricity
- sound
- chemical

All energy is classed as either potential energy or kinetic energy. Potential energy is stored energy, as in a battery. Kinetic energy is the energy of motion, as in a moving, battery-operated toy. The potential energy in the battery gets changed to the kinetic energy of the toy.

Quick fact

The metric unit of both work and energy is the **joule (J)**. A joule is the amount of energy exerted by a force of one newton (1 N) applied over a distance of one meter (1 m).

Electrical Energy

Imagine what your life would be like without electricity. In large part, Western society is powered by electric energy. Over the last 250 years, inventors have developed many electricity sources, including coal, natural gas, nuclear fission, and hydroelectric. Much research today explores clean, renewable sources of energy such as the motion of the wind and tides as well as solar energy.

↑ *These solar panels convert energy from the Sun (solar energy) into electrical energy.*

Thermal Energy

Thermal energy, transferred as heat, is the energy of molecules in motion. Thermal energy always moves from a warmer spot to a colder one. There are three ways in which thermal energy is transferred.

- *Conduction:* Have you ever picked up an all-metal fork by the handle when the tines had been left on the barbecue for an hour? The handle becomes very hot. Hot, energetic molecules in the tines collided with slower, cooler ones in the handle, and conducted (transferred) their heat.
- *Convection:* Thermal energy can be transferred by the flow of gases or liquids as well. A pot of water starting to boil illustrates the transfer of heat by convection. The water at the bottom, nearest the element, becomes less dense and rises. Its thermal energy istransferred to cooler water.
- *Radiation:* Radiation is the only type of heat transfer that requires no medium or mass. The Sun radiates light and heat to the Earth through empty space.

Quick fact

Friction can be used to generate electricity. The first "friction machines" were developed in the late 1600s. Newton himself suggested an improvement to early designs.

"The most convincing proof of the conversion of heat into living force...has been derived from my experiments with the electromagnetic engine, a machine composed of magnets and bars of iron set in motion by an electrical battery. I have proved by actual experiment that, in exact proportion to the force with which this machine works, heat is abstracted from the electrical battery."

—James Prescott Joule

↑These windmills convert the kinetic energy of wind into electrical energy.

Did You Know?

Friction results in the kinetic energy of motion being converted into thermal energy. You are using friction to generate thermal energy when you rub your hands together to warm them up.

James Prescott Joule

James Prescott Joule (1818–1889) was an English physicist. His research on the relationships among electrical, mechanical, and chemical effects led to the first law of thermodynamics. That law states that the amount of energy in the universe is constant. Energy can be stored, changed in form, or relocated, but it cannot be created or destroyed.

Joule also described heat mathematically as a form of energy. The metric unit of energy, the joule, is named in his honor. His careful measurements came to be regarded as a model for good scientific practice.

CHAPTER SEVEN

The Cutting Edge

Isaac Newton's three laws of motion, along with his law of universal law of gravitation, helped people make sense of the universe. But they are not his only contributions to science.

Newton also helped define experimental methods in physics. His approach meant that scientists could more easily understand, assess, and learn from each others' work. He expressed his findings in mathematical terms, so that they could be applied as widely as possible.

In addition to these achievements, Newton is famous for pioneering in two other areas. He was one of the founders of **calculus**, and he formulated laws that reliably describe rotating motion and color in light.

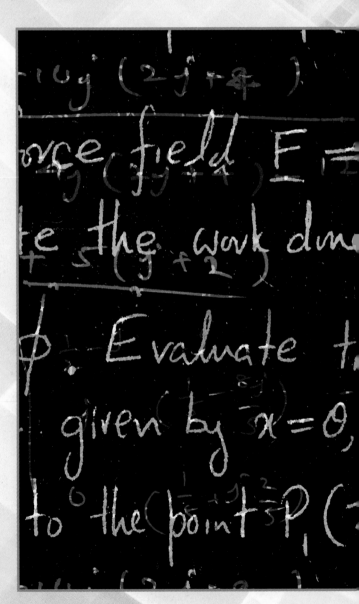

→ Newton and Leibniz both developed notations for calculus. Today mathematicians use notations based on Leibniz's system.

Calculus: A Mathematics of Motion

Also known as real analysis, calculus is a form of mathematics that can describe change. Calculus is ideally suited to calculations involving acceleration, velocity, mass, and work. In other words, it is ideally suited to calculations involving the laws of motion. It has many other applications, too. Newton developed and used methods of calculus in the *Principia*.

Integral calculus enables us to determine the surface area and volume of spheres and cones, or the surface area under a curve. Differential calculus determines the rate of change in a system, for example, the rate of acceleration of a skydiver.

Quick fact

Gottfried Leibniz (1646–1716) and Isaac Newton argued fiercely for 15 years over which of them should get the credit for developing calculus. Today, they are given equal credit.

Spinning Tops Grow Up to be Gyroscopes

How does a toy spinning top manage to whirl on its axis for 15 seconds or more without falling? Galileo and Newton wondered about this, and spent much time studying tops. The spinning motion itself keeps the top stable and upright. Eventually, however, friction slows the top down. This reduces the stabilizing effect of the spinning. The center of gravity gets lower and lower and eventually gravity wins—and the top falls down.

The principle underlying the top has practical uses. The **gyroscope**—a more complicated form of top—tells us when a moving object has changed direction. In that way, gyroscopes help keep watercraft and aircraft headed in the right direction.

The spinning wheel of a gyroscope can be set inside two or more circular frames. Each frame is oriented along a different axis. No matter what angle the framework tilts at, the spinning wheel keeps its position. It can thus provide information about direction.

←*Modern day gyroscopes have many applications. One example is to aid navigation in mine tunnels.*

Newton's Experiments with Light and Prisms

Imagination is a critical tool of science. We can see this in the true tale of the spinning top that became the gyroscope of navigation. Scientists who wonder about simple things or play with simple toys sometimes come away with ideas about nature. These ideas can lead to more new ideas and eventually to technologies that transform our lives.

Newton became interested in the motion of light and its effects. He was able to establish some key facts: If an apple is red, that is not because it absorbs red rays and reflects all the other colors. Quite the opposite is true, in fact. Red is the color the apple reflects. The other rays are absorbed.

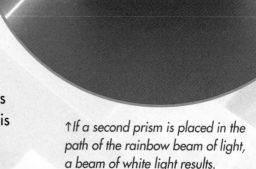

↑If a second prism is placed in the path of the rainbow beam of light, a beam of white light results.

How Prisms Work

How do **prisms** break up white light into colors? Waves of light travel through the air into the prism. Glass differs from air in its ability to make waves bend (its refractive index). As it enters the glass, the light bends. But the angle of the bend is different for the different colors of light. Thus, the light "spreads out" and exits the prism as a rainbow. When natural rainbows form after a downpour, suspended droplets of rain act as prisms.

In Newton's time, many people thought that sunlight was white and that the prism produced the colors we see. By a simple experiment he showed instead that sunlight is a blend of all the colors of the spectrum. He first separated the colors into the familiar rainbow band, using a prism, and then rejoined them, using a second prism. The result was white light again.

Triangular prisms are not merely amusements or ornaments. They are a necessary part of scientific instruments such as the spectroscope. The spectroscope tells us what elements distant stars consist of, by producing a spectrum of their light.

The Reflecting Telescope

The telescope was invented in about 1608, probably in Holland. But ahead of the astronomers of the day lay centuries of trial and error. At that time, to prevent distorted images, astronomical telescopes had to be very long, sometimes 200 feet (61 m). In 1668, Isaac Newton built the first **reflecting telescope**. He used a concave (cup-shaped) silver mirror to give an image with less distortion than with other telescopes.

←Completed in 1987, the William Herschel telescope shown here is one of three reflecting telescopes in the Isaac Newton Group of Telescopes. The telescopes are found in the Canary Islands and are used in astronomical research.

The Limits of Newton's Laws

Newton's laws apply across the Earth and universe except in two areas—the very great and the very small. Albert Einstein 1879–1955) showed in 1905 that objects do not follow the laws of motion when approaching the speed of light. Light travels faster than anything else we know of with a speed of 186,000 miles per second (300,000,000 m/s). Other researchers discovered that the very small particles that make up atoms do not follow the laws of motion either. So classical mechanics was not a complete system after all. The universe was not the clockwork system it had seemed to be.

Albert Einstein and Newton's Ideas

Newton thought that space and time were absolute, universal, and independent of how objects move. In his famous 1905 papers, Einstein introduced his theory of relativity, in which space and time are relative to the observer.

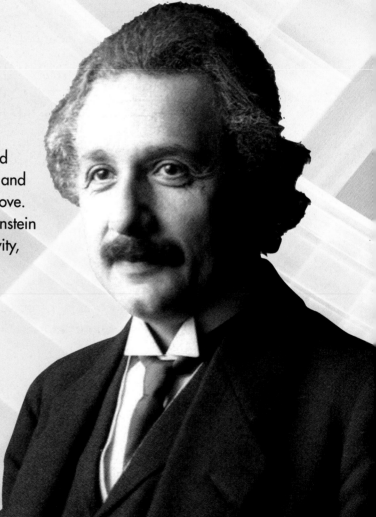

→ *German-born Albert Einstein, like Newton, revolutionized science with his ideas.*

Einstein's Theory of Relativity

Special relativity deals with inertial frames of reference. **Inertial** means having constant motion. Einstein said that the speed of light remained constant, regardless of the observer's frame of reference. This results in many strange predictions for frames of reference at high speeds, such as the warping of length of objects and time. Scientists have since proven these predictions experimentally.

General relativity says that very large objects such as galaxies cause time and space to bend. Then they may not appear to obey Newton's laws of motion. If, for example, you put a bowling ball on a soft mattress, it bends the mattress. So if you applied Newton's laws to motion in the curve because you assumed it was really straight, your predictions would not be accurate.

↑ Einstein's theory of general relativity predicted that light would bend near large galaxies. Today, astronomers take this "gravitational lensing" into account when studying far-off galaxies.

Einstein's theory of relativity completely changed the way physicists thought about time, space, motion, mass, and gravity. His most famous equation, $E = mc^2$ (energy equals mass times the velocity of light squared), underlies the development of atomic energy.

The Weird World of Quantum Physics

Quantum physics, or quantum mechanics, is the study of how **subatomic particles** behave. Three things that twentieth century physicists learned about them would surprise Newton:

- Quantities of energy jump from one level to the next with nothing in between. Newton and other early scientists assumed that there would be many stages in between as energy changed, perhaps an infinite number.
- Light behaves like particles sometimes (as Newton had assumed). At other times it behaves like waves.
- We can never determine both a particle's momentum and its position at the same time.
- Understanding quantum physics makes the laser, the electron microscope, and magnetic resonance imaging possible.

Today, scientists use **particle accelerators** (once called "atom smashers") to speed up particles to the speed of light and then aim them at atoms, to break them up and study them.

Looking into the atom, they made many key discoveries. They learned, for example, of other forces in the universe besides gravity and electromagnetism (electricity and magnetism), which earlier scientists had identified.

The **strong nuclear force**—stronger than electricity or gravity—holds together the positively charged protons in an atom's nucleus. Otherwise, they would repel each other and atoms would fly apart. Particles called **gluons** provide the force. They are called gluons because they "glue" other particles together.

New Horizons

People tend to think we know how nature works, based on our own observations and the science of our day. But we can be mistaken even when our views are reasonable, and based on observation and evidence. Without the questioning spirit of science, people would still think the Earth is flat. They would still believe the Sun revolves around the Earth. Newton was not afraid to question and overturn accepted ideas. His work not only gave us better knowledge about the world, but paved the way for useful theories, discoveries, and inventions that help shape our society today. His questioning approach to the universe also helped shape the face of modern science.

↑ Space travel is possible due to the work of Newton, as well as the scientists who came before and after him.

"Equipped with his five senses, man explores the universe around him and calls the adventure Science."

— astronomer Edwin Hubble
(1889–1953)

Timeline

428 B.C.–348 B.C.	Plato teaches that the planets, the Sun, and other stars (heavenly bodies) moved, along with the Moon, in perfect circles around an Earth fixed in place.
384 B.C.–322 B.C.	Aristotle teaches that rotating spheres carry planets around in their orbits.
287 B.C.–212 B.C.	Archimedes improves on the hydraulic screw, an Egyptian invention used to raise water from one level to another.
276 B.C.–194 B.C.	Eratosthenes measures the circumference of Earth quite accurately for his time.
127–141	Ptolemy predicts the motions of the planets accurately, without a telescope. But he assumes that Earth is at the center of the solar system.
1543	Nicolaus Copernicus proposes that the Sun is fixed in the center of the universe and that Earth and other planets revolve around it.
1564–1642	Galileo Galilei designs and carries out experiments to find out about the nature of the world.
1584	Galileo develops the law of the pendulum, describing the motion of rolling bodies.
1596	Galileo invents a military compass that aims cannonballs accurately.
1604	Astronomers observe a supernova (exploding star), which shows that stars can change—a new idea.
1608	The telescope is invented in Holland.
1609	Johannes Kepler publishes a description of the three laws of planetary motion.
1610	Galileo observes phases of Venus, the craters on the Moon, and the moons of Jupiter through a telescope.
1611	A number of astronomers, including Galileo, see sunspots.
1616	Galileo is told not to believe, discuss, or defend the Copernican (sun-centered) model of the universe as fact.
1632	Galileo is summoned to Rome and interrogated, under threat of torture, for defending the Copernican model as fact.

1633	Galileo is sentenced to house arrest for life, but continues to publish.
1642	Isaac Newton is born in Lincolnshire, England.
1642–1727	Newton continues Galileo's experiments and integrates mathematics closely with science.
1668	Newton develops a reflecting telescope.
1669	Newton is named Lucasian Professor of Mathematics at Cambridge University.
1687	Newton publishes the *Principia*, which describes his three laws of motion and the law of universal gravitation.
1704	Newton publishes *Optics*, on the science of light.
1705	Newton is knighted by Queen Anne.
1727	Newton dies at his home in London.
1803	Thomas Young demonstrates that light travels as waves.
1807	Thomas Young is the first to use the term "energy."
1834	The term "scientist" is first recorded. Before that, most people doing what we would today call science were called natural philosophers.
1849	James Prescott Joule states the first law of thermodynamics.
1900	Respected British scientist William Thomson Kelvin announces in a keynote lecture that all important science problems are solved.
1905	Albert Einstein shows that Newton's laws do not account for the motion of heavenly bodies over large distances.
1913	Niels Bohr constructs a theory of atoms based on quantum mechanics.
1927	Werner Heisenberg formulates the uncertainty principle, which says that you cannot know with precision both a particle's momentum and its position.
1992	The Catholic Church apologizes for its treatment of Galileo.
2010	The Google search engine celebrates Isaac Newton's birthday by adding an animated falling apple to its logo.

Glossary

acceleration The rate of change of velocity over time

astrology The study of the movements of the planets and stars with the belief that they influence natural events and the course of human lives

astronomy The scientific study of objects such as planets, stars, and galaxies in outer space

calculus A form of mathematics; one kind of calculus is used to analyze change in systems or processes, another can be applied to determine areas and volumes

center of gravity The average location of the weight of an object (the downward force that gravity exerts)

classical mechanics The study of the effects of energy and forces on physical objects; based on Newton's laws of motion

counterfeit A fake copy of something

density The quantity of mass in a given volume

directly proportional Increasing or decreasing together; two variables are said to be directly proportional if, when one increases, the other increases as well

drag The "stopping" force created when an object moves through a liquid or gas

element For Aristotle, earth, water, air, and fire. In today's science, an element is a substance that cannot be broken down to a simpler substance by chemical processes.

energy The ability to do work; measured in joules (J)

force A push or pull on an object

friction The "stopping" force created when two solid objects are in contact

general relativity A general theory of time and space that combines special relativity and classical mechanics to provide a geometric view of gravitation

gluon A subatomic particle thought to bind subatomic particles such as quarks, antiquarks, and gluons themselves to one another

gravity The attraction between two masses, such as the Earth and an object on its surface

gyroscope A tool of navigation that provides information about direction

hieroglyphs Pictorial symbols used to represent meaning, sounds, or both in written language such as that of the ancient Egyptians

hypothesis A testable explanation about how nature works; before it becomes widely accepted and supported by evidence, a theory starts out as a hypothesis

inertia The resistance of objects to changes in their motion

inertial Of a time frame, having constant motion

inversely proportional Increasing or decreasing oppositely; two quantities are said to be inversely proportional if, when one increases, the other decreases and vice versa.

joule (J) Metric unit of energy; equivalent to the force of one newton applied over a displacement of one meter

law of the pendulum For a given pendulum, the time it takes for a swing (the period) is the same, regardless of the size of the swing.

mass The quantity of matter ("stuff") in an object

momentum A measure of an object's tendency to keep moving; the mass of an object multiplied by its velocity

motion The process of changing position; movement

newton (N) The unit of measurement of force. A force of one newton (1 N) will accelerate a mass of 2.2 lbs (1 kg) at the rate of 39 inches (1 m) per second per second.

parabola A particular kind of curve; describes the path of projectiles in motion

particle accelerator A device that accelerates atoms or subatomic particles to very high speeds

prism A triangular piece of clear glass or plastic; used in experiments with light

projectile An object thrown, fired, or otherwise driven forward, such as a baseball thrown by a pitcher

quantum mechanics (quantum physics) Theory and laws used to study and explain the behavior of subatomic particles

reflecting telescope A telescope that uses one or more curved mirrors to correct distortions created by the lens

relativity Einstein's revolutionary theory; see special relativity and general relativity

scientific law A statement that describes a pattern in nature. It may be a statement in words, a mathematical equation, or both.

scientific theory An explanation for observations of the natural world; supported by a great deal of evidence

special relativity Einstein's theory about the relationship of time and space to the frame of reference of the observer

strong nuclear force Holds together protons and neutrons in an atom's nucleus

subatomic particles Parts smaller than an atom. Neutrons, electrons, and protons are the three main subatomic particles.

theorem In mathematics, a statement that has been proven true via a proof

thermal energy The energy of particles in motion; transfer of thermal energy is called heat.

vacuum The absence of matter in a given space

velocity The speed of an object and its direction of travel

weight The force with which an object is attracted by gravity; "heaviness"

work Energy transferred by a force acting over a distance; measured in joules (J)

For More Information

Books

Bow, James. **Cycling Science.** Crabtree Publishing, 2009.

Green, Jen. **Hail! Ancient Greeks.** Crabtree Publishing, 2010.

Jefferis, David. **Star Spotters: Telescopes and Observatories.** Crabtree Publishing, 2009.

Krull, Kathleen. **Isaac Newton.** Penguin Group, 2006.

Steele, Philip. **Isaac Newton: The Scientist Who Changed Everything.** National Geographic Society, 2007.

Websites

www.brainpop.com/science/motionsandforces/newtonslawsofmotion/preview.weml
Watch an animation that shows Newton's laws of motion in action.

http://science.discovery.com/interactives/literacy/newton/newton.html
Clever animations demonstrate each of Newton's three laws. Take the quiz after you watch!

www.physics4kids.com/files/motion_intro.html
Here you'll find in-depth descriptions of the laws of motion, forces, friction, gravity, and more.

www.pbs.org/opb/circus/classroom/circus-physics/newtons-laws/
Circus dogs demonstrate Newton's laws in this entertaining video.

www.newtonproject.sussex.ac.uk/
You can find all of Newton's writings online here.

Index